Inside the World's Most Infamous Terrorist Organizations

The Irish Republican Army

Susie Derkins

The Rosen Publishing Group, Inc.
New York

To Annie Hogan

Published in 2003 by The Rosen Publishing Group, Inc.
29 East 21st Street, New York, NY 10010

First Edition

Library of Congress Cataloging-in-Publication Data

Derkins, Susie.
The Irish Republican Army / Susie Derkins. — 1st ed.
    p. cm. — (Inside the world's most infamous terrorist organizations)
Summary: Examines the historical origins, philosophy, and most notorious attacks of the Irish Republican Army (IRA) and discusses their present activities and counter-terrorism efforts directed against them.
Includes bibliographical references and index.
ISBN 0-8239-3822-0
1. Irish Republican Army—History—Juvenile literature. 2. Ireland—History—20th century—Juvenile literature. 3. Political violence—Northern Ireland—Juvenile literature. 4. Political violence—Ireland—Juvenile literature. 5. Northern Ireland—History—Juvenile literature. 6. Guerrilla warfare—Juvenile literature. 7. Terrorism—Juvenile literature. [1. Irish Republican Army—History. 2. Northern Ireland—History. 3. Political violence. 4. Terrorism.]
I. Title. II. Series.
DA914.D47 2002
941.50824—dc21

                                                                    2002010759

Manufactured in the United States of America

Contents

Introduction

The group that would become the Irish Republican Army (IRA) began to emerge in 1916 to advocate Irish sovereignty, or freedom from British rule. The British had occupied Ireland for more than 800 years, often treating the native Irish Catholics with extreme brutality and harsh discrimination.

In the 1920s, Ireland was partitioned (split in two) after it lost the War of Independence with Britain. The Government of Ireland Act of 1920 (not fully ratified until January 1922) officially split the country between twenty-six counties in the south—the Free State of Ireland (and later, in 1949, the Republic of Ireland)—and the six counties in the north—Northern Ireland. The British ruled Northern Ireland, while the Free State had its government, which operated largely free of British interference. Perhaps most significantly, the Irish living in the Free State could freely practice their Catholic religion, something their northern cousins were not permitted to do.

In the north, Irish Catholics were not given the same opportunities for jobs or housing as Irish Protestants were. They were also treated unfairly by the police and the military, often being rounded up and brutalized with little or no justification. Catholics who remained in Northern Ireland felt as though they were unwelcome criminals in their own homeland. The partitioning of the country was (and remains) unacceptable to Irish Republicans. Irish Republicans, such as IRA members, make it their objective to fight

Catholic Republicans march in a parade organized by the Irish Republican Army in April 1966. Because of the long history of oppression and discrimination against Catholics, the IRA, despite its violent and radical tactics, has often been able to inspire loyal allegiance among a broad swath of the population—rural farmers and urban businesspeople, men and women, old and young.

for a thirty-two-county, independent republic of Ireland, and many are willing to use violence to achieve that goal.

The IRA was founded with the purpose of fighting for the civil liberties of all residents of the thirty-two counties. Its members sought to obtain religious freedoms, civil rights, and equal opportunities for all Irish people, and to mend the divisions between the north and south that festered under British rule. Despite its noble intentions, however, the battle the IRA undertook and the tactics it used were controversial from the start.

The IRA's presence remains strong in many neighborhoods of Northern Ireland, despite its cease-fire and the reduced numbers of British troops in the six counties. The group offers Catholics protection against active Protestant paramilitary groups.

IRA members arm themselves with weapons and are willing to use them if they feel it is necessary to achieve their political goals or to defend their community. Like most politically extremist groups, the IRA took dramatic—and often deadly—action in order to make their beliefs heard. Not all Irish Republicans are sympathetic to the IRA. Some people believe that the IRA commits mindless acts of violence and that its members are criminals, if not terrorists.

Most IRA attacks have been directed against British troops, police officers, government officials, military outposts, Protestant paramilitary groups, and other representatives of British authority. Innocent civilians, however, have often been inadvertently killed by IRA actions. Sometimes they were even the intended targets of IRA bombings. The historic events that gave rise to this embrace of violence by Irish Republicans are complicated and far-reaching. An examination of the political history of Ireland is necessary to understand the hatred and violence that grip Catholics and Protestants.

The Political History of Ireland

The English conquest of Ireland began in the twelfth century when the Normans (who had earlier come from modern-day France to conquer the Anglo-Saxons in England) first arrived in Ireland. These English settlers soon adopted the native Irish ways, however, and the English Crown gained little control over the island. During the sixteenth century and the Protestant reigns of Henry VIII and Elizabeth I, the English did finally gain authority and control over all of Ireland and began to suppress Catholicism. Under King James I, settlers from England and Scotland were encouraged to immigrate to Ireland with generous offers to buy parcels of the country's best farmland. The native Irish clans that had been living on this land were kicked off, or dispossessed. Their ancestral lands (and the only source of sustenance and wealth in a mostly rural and agricultural country) were taken away and given to the newly arrived British colonists.

Interaction between the native Irish population and the newcomers was difficult and strained. The newcomers spoke English rather than the Irish language, Gaelic. Perhaps most significant, most of the newcomers, like their king, were Protestant, while the native people were mostly Catholic. Backed by the king and his army, the Protestants quickly gained political power over the dispossessed Irish.

1

CHAPTER

7

The Great Potato Famine

The often impoverished and oppressed Irish Catholics would be visited by an even greater calamity in the mid-nineteenth century. The Great Potato Famine, also known as the Great Hunger or Great Famine, struck the people of rural Ireland from 1845 to 1852. It began in the summer of 1845, when a fungus known as the black rot spread throughout the farmlands of Ireland, completely destroying the potato crop.

Following the dispossession of native Irish farmers, landowners in Ireland at the time of the famine were mostly British and Protestant and often absentee—they owned the land but lived elsewhere and rented the fields to Irish Catholic tenants. The Irish tenant farmers who lived and worked on the landowners' properties depended on the potato crop for survival. Potatoes provided both sustenance and money to pay the rent.

In the absence of a plentiful potato harvest, the price of other kinds of food soared dramatically. Farmers couldn't find money to feed themselves much less pay rent. As a result, landlords evicted (forced from the land) hundreds of thousands of people. Most of these poor Irish farmers and their families had no choice but to move to disease-ridden workhouses (government-run institutions where people who could not pay their debts were sent to perform menial labor). Many of the starving Irish immigrated to America. Hundreds of thousands of sick, desperate people crowded onto ships that lost up to a third of their passengers to disease and starvation even before reaching port. The death rates were so high that the boats came to be referred to as "coffin ships."

By the time the Great Famine ended, more than one million Irish people had died from starvation. A million and a half more

A mural in a Republican area of Belfast, Northern Ireland, depicting the Great Potato Famine. Murals are a popular form of propaganda and cultural expression among both Protestants and Catholics in Northern Ireland. They also provide a way to preserve and relate—on a daily basis—the troubled history of the Irish people. More than a century and a half later, the Potato Famine remains a deeply sad and emotionally charged chapter in Ireland's history, particularly for the Catholic population.

were forced to leave Ireland just to survive. Most of them migrated to the United States and Canada. Many peasants who remained ate the rotten potatoes and became deathly ill with diseases such as cholera and typhus. Others were found dead in roadside ditches, their mouths grass-stained. They had been reduced to eating grass in a last desperate attempt to ward off starvation.

While the British government provided some financial support to the starving peasants of Ireland, many of them felt that Britain did not help quickly enough. Many people also blamed centuries of political oppression for the conditions that allowed the famine to occur in the first place. If the Irish Catholics had not been kicked off their land and forced to live in extreme poverty, the crop failure would have been painful, but it would not have led to mass starvation, disease, and death. The people of Ireland were unarmed when the famine began; otherwise widespread violence may have erupted. As it was, there were only sporadic, spontaneous, and isolated acts of aggression. The horrifying and devastating legacy of the Great Famine, however, caused many Irish citizens to seek dramatic political and social change, through violent means if necessary.

Almost half a century would pass before Irish Republicans made an attempt at armed resistance. In the meantime, the fight for independence was waged through peaceful, legitimate means—in the form of campaigns for constitutional land reform (which would reduce rents and compensate tenant farmers who had been evicted by landlords). When the Irish Party participated in the British House of Commons, it represented the overwhelming majority of Irish people, who strongly desired complete independence from British rule. They pushed for Home Rule legislation that would allow the Irish limited self-government, while Ireland would remain

Police charge demonstrators who carry banners reading, "No Home Rule" during the Belfast riots of 1886. The riots began as news of the Home Rule Bill's defeat came through. Catholics clashed with Protestant Loyalists, and Loyalists clashed with police as bonfires and burning tar barrels blazed throughout the city. The conflict raged all through the summer, officially resulting in thirty-one deaths (though the actual death toll is thought to be closer to fifty).

within the British Empire. Even though this fell far short of Irish independence and represented a compromise position, the Home Rule legislation was defeated by the British Parliament in both 1886 and 1893. Independence—even a highly watered-down version—continued to elude the people of Ireland.

The Struggle for Home Rule

Irish patriots continued to fight for independence through legal means and legitimate political channels for the rest of the nineteenth century. Finally, in 1912, the British Liberal government passed a Home Rule bill in the House of Commons, the lower house of England's two-chamber Parliament. Although this meant that some limited form of self-government for Ireland was finally possible, the desire of the overwhelming majority of Irish people for a united republic and religious and political freedom for all was still not granted. Home Rule would not end British rule or taxation. Instead, it would set up an Irish legislature that had control over domestic matters and place Irish representatives who could vote on issues related to Irish taxation in the British Parliament.

The bill's most controversial provision centered on law enforcement. Ever since Ireland was conquered in the sixteenth century, Britain had policed the country with its armed forces. Under Home Rule, the British would eventually hand control of the police forces over to the Irish. Irish Protestants were alarmed by this switchover, fearing domination by Catholics and the possible loss of their land, homes, and livelihoods. As a result, they began forming private armies, including the Ulster Volunteer Force (UVF). These Protestant militias were prepared to use force, if necessary, to fight Home Rule.

The political situation became even worse very quickly. Angered over the passage of Home Rule, the British Parliament's Conservative Party joined with the Irish Unionists (also referred to as Loyalists)—pro-British, Protestant Irish citizens who were anti–Home Rule. Together they exerted pressure on Parliament's upper—and more conservative—chamber, the House of Lords, to reject Home Rule.

English Liberal prime minister William Ewart Gladstone (1809–1898) delivers his last speech in the House of Commons on February 23, 1893, arguing in favor of his Irish Home Rule bill. The bill passed in the House of Commons but was defeated in the House of Lords. The controversial bill had created a split in his own party, and Gladstone resigned from office in March 1894. He died at Hawarden, England, on May 19, 1898.

At the time, there was little organization among Irish Republicans. To their horror, however, they saw many British aristocrats and leading members of the Conservative Party openly encourage the Unionists to engage in armed rebellion against Home Rule. The UVF was even allowed to freely import weapons into Ireland in preparation for revolt, smuggling in 24,000 rifles and hundreds of thousands of rounds of ammunition. When the Liberal government made plans to use the British army to quash the UVF, senior British officers refused to participate, so the Liberals were forced to back down. The open and democratic process that resulted in passage of the Home Rule Bill was undermined by threats of violence, while the Catholics in Ireland continued to suffer discrimination and oppression in their own land.

The IRA's Roots

To counter the British-Unionist alliance and its threat of violence, the Irish Volunteers (or in Gaelic, Oglaigh na hEireann) was established in 1913. The Irish Volunteers would eventually evolve into the Irish Republican Army.

By 1914, the Irish Volunteers numbered about 100,000. Like the UVF, they began importing weapons in preparation for an armed battle over Home Rule. Unlike the UVF, however, the British government did not turn a blind eye to their activities. While trying to import only a small number of rifles at Howth Harbor, outside Dublin, they were attacked by British forces who tried but failed to stop the smugglers, who escaped. Angry and frustrated, the British troops marched back into Dublin and fired into a crowd of civilians, killing three. The shootings may have been the result of an officer's hand gesture that was misinterpreted as an order to open fire.

When World War I began in Europe later in 1914, Home Rule had again been passed in the British House of Commons, and it became law in September 1914. It was suspended due to the war, however, and was never reinstated.

The Birth
of the IRA

A long history of oppression and poverty fueled the anger and discontent of the Catholic Irish in the early twentieth century. For hundreds of years, they had been unwilling subjects of the British empire, and for most of that time, they had fought unsuccessfully to regain their independence. The biggest grievance the Catholic Irish had against their British rulers was the unfair political treatment they received. The Irish Parliament was inadequate and inefficient. It had no real power to represent Irish people within the British government. In addition, Britain ruled Ireland in the same manner that it governed all of its colonies—it acted according to what would best serve Britain's interests, not those of the occupied land.

The religious oppression of Catholic people in Ireland was also a cause for great anger. The majority of Irish people were, and still are, Catholic. Nevertheless, Irish Catholics were systematically denied religious freedom by the British government. Britain forbade Irish Catholics from practicing their religion and providing education for their own children. Catholic people were not even allowed to be teachers. But Irish parents could not send their children outside of Ireland for education without forfeiting their land and their citizenship.

2
CHAPTER

British soldiers and Irish Republicans shoot at each other on a narrow, smoke-filled street as an overturned cart burns in Dublin, Ireland, during the Easter Rebellion of April 1916. Inset: British soldiers shoot from behind a barricade of empty beer casks in Dublin during the Easter Rebellion.

The Easter Rebellion

Feelings of anger that had been brewing for decades came to a peak on April 24, 1916—Easter Monday—in Ireland's capital city of Dublin. On that day, some 1,500 men—mostly members of the Irish Volunteers, the Irish Republican Brotherhood (a secretive militant organization), and a radical labor group called the Citizen Army—seized the city through military force. They were led by Padraic Pearse, a poet, political activist, and Gaelic newspaper editor; socialist leader James Connolly; and poet Thomas MacDonagh. The men blockaded the Dublin post office and barricaded surrounding streets using sandbags and barbed wire.

After capturing the city, the leaders of the Easter Rebellion declared Ireland independent. In open defiance of British rule, they raised the Irish flag above the city. Then the men signed the Proclamation of the Republic. The proclamation called for an independent, united Irish Republic and "equal rights and equal opportunities" for all Irish people. Pearse was named president of this new republic, and Connolly was named commander general of its army. By the next day, the rebels had the majority of Dublin under their control.

The British quickly launched a counterattack. British troops arrived in Dublin, and bloody battles erupted in the streets. From the roofs of nearby houses, Republican snipers shot at British soldiers. More than 100 civilian deaths were reported, while the British lost more than 400 troops. Almost 200 buildings in Dublin, including the homes of private citizens, were destroyed. Outnumbered and with far less weaponry, the Irish rebels were no match for the British military forces. Realizing that they had no chance for military victory, they surrendered on April 29.

As punishment for participation in the Easter Rebellion, sixteen people were killed by the British government. Rebel leaders such as Pearse, Connolly, and MacDonagh were executed by firing squad. Many civilian participants in the Easter Rebellion received life imprisonment.

Sinn Féin

In the wake of the Easter Rebellion and the execution of its leaders, many Irish people found themselves privately sympathetic to a group now calling itself the Irish Republican Army, formed from the remnants of various rebel groups that had participated in the rebellion, including the Irish Volunteers. Many Irish Catholics supported the IRA's cause, if not the frequently bloody means by which the rebels attempted to achieve their goals. In the general election of 1918, these people had an opportunity to vote for a legitimate political party that promised to fight—in the halls of Parliament—the same fight the IRA was waging in the streets.

Sinn Féin (Gaelic for "ourselves alone" or "we ourselves") was formed as a formal political party in Ireland in 1905. It argued for British withdrawal from Ireland and the formation of an independent republic. In 1918, Sinn Féin won a large majority in the general election riding the tide of public opinion that had risen following the Easter Rebellion. The following year, armed with this popular support, Sinn Féin established an independent Irish parliament, called Dáil Éireann, and declared Ireland's sovereignty as a united republic. Independent institutions—a central government, administrative bodies, and courts of law—were created. The Irish Volunteers were renamed the Army of the Republic and were designated the military wing of the new republic. This was

Arthur Griffith, one of the founders of Sinn Féin, was born in Dublin on March 31, 1872, and was a printer by trade. He developed a passionate interest in Irish history and culture and became active in the Gaelic League while serving as editor of several radical newspapers. In 1905, he helped establish Sinn Féin. In 1921 he accepted the responsibility of leading a delegation to London to negotiate the treaty that established the Irish Free State and separated Northern Ireland from the rest of the country. Griffith was elected first president of the Free State's new legislature, the Dáil Éireann, in January 1922, but he died on August 12 of that year, shortly after the outbreak of the Irish civil war between those who accepted partition and those who opposed it.

Sinn Féin and the IRA

Before their executions by firing squad for participation in the Easter Rebellion, Pearse and Connolly, as well as several other rebel leaders, were members of Sinn Féin. Ever since the Easter Rebellion, Sinn Féin has been linked with the IRA and widely considered the secret political arm of the group.

Officially, the relationship between Sinn Féin and the IRA is only symbolic and philosophical—both have stated for the record that they are totally unrelated organizations. Many Irish Republicans who oppose the IRA's violent tactics nevertheless support the Sinn Féin party. In the minds of most people, however, Sinn Féin is the political wing of the Irish Republican Army, and supporting it means an implied approval of the IRA's violent tactics.

an incredibly defiant and dangerous provocation, as none of these activities were permitted by the British government. They amounted to an open act of rebellion, not unlike the American colonies' declaration of independence 150 years earlier.

Martial Law and Guerrilla Warfare

The response from the British government to Sinn Féin's defiant acts was swift and angry. It banned the new institutions and declared war on the new Irish republic. Mayors of three Irish cities—all of whom were members of the IRA—were executed by British troops. Martial law was declared throughout most of Ireland. (Martial law is the sending of military forces into an occupied territory by a government after civilian law enforcement—such as the police—fails to maintain control.) Shops, factories, and even homes of innocent people were burned to the ground.

The IRA quickly responded with an effective guerrilla campaign against the British occupying forces that resulted in several dozen deaths of military and police officers and civilians in 1920. A guerrilla fighter engages in irregular warfare—acts of harassment or sabotage such as bombings, ambushes, raids, assassinations, and street fights—and often operates as a member of an independent unit, or cell. The advantage of a cell structure is that it allows small groups of people to plan various and separate attacks simultaneously. It also makes it harder for the authorities to do more than shut down a cell or two at a time. Since members of one cell are often unaware of the plans and identities of members of other cells, they cannot provide the authorities with information on the group during interrogation. The activities and membership of the group as a whole will remain largely secretive.

These guerrilla tactics seemed to work. The British expressed interest in negotiating with Irish leaders. When the IRA was not pressed to surrender its arms, its leaders agreed to negotiate with the British government. The two factions declared a truce in July 1921. The result of the following negotiations would sever Ireland in two, creating a raw wound that has yet to heal.

Partition and Civil War

While the IRA's guerrilla campaign had forced the British government into negotiations with the Irish, the outcome of these discussions would cause a serious fracture among Irish nationalists. Two months after negotiations toward an Anglo-Irish treaty began, an agreement was signed on December 6, 1921. Its terms stated that the

The June 1922 arrest of Reginald Dunne and Joseph O'Sullivan immediately after the assassination by two IRA gunmen of Sir Henry Wilson, a British field marshal and security adviser to the government of the newly established Northern Ireland. Wilson's assassination helped spark the Irish civil war by provoking a crackdown on Republicans by the government of the Irish Free State.

twenty-six southern counties would become the independent Irish Free State while the six northern counties would remain part of the United Kingdom, subject to British rule. In effect, the southern and largely Catholic counties were being separated from the northern, Protestant counties. While it was hoped that this would calm sectarian tension by creating a free Catholic Irish state (where Catholics from the north could resettle), it also closed the door to the possibility of a united, independent, whole Ireland—the long-held dream of Irish Republicans.

In January 1922, the Dáil Éireann voted 64–57 in favor of the treaty, but the debate was extremely bitter. Those who voted in favor were accused of being traitors to Ireland. Among those opposed to the treaty were members of the IRA who could not accept partition and its partial offer of independence. Instead, the group planned to achieve independence for all of Ireland through military means, taking action without consulting the Republican politicians they felt had betrayed the cause.

Their first strike was the assassination of Sir Henry Wilson, a British field marshal and security adviser to the new government of Northern Ireland. In an attempt to quash this guerrilla activity, the Free State government cracked down on those opposed to the Anglo-Irish treaty. Instead of restoring calm, full-scale civil war broke out in the south. The IRA orchestrated bombings, raids, and street battles on both sides of the new border separating the Free State from Northern Ireland. During the civil war, close to 5,000 people were killed before hostilities finally ended in May 1923 with the Free State government emerging as the victor. The IRA commanded its members to lay down their arms.

A Temporary Lull

Throughout the next forty years, the IRA entered a less active period. It began to weaken due to disagreements within the group. It also began to lose popularity as a result of its violent tactics and support of Germany during World War II. In addition, many Irish Catholics living in the south felt that the Republic of Ireland, as the Free State became known in 1949, was victory enough. Though composed of only twenty-six counties, it was now entirely free of allegiance to the British Crown. Finally, having been outlawed by both Irish governments, the IRA was forced to become a secret organization, hindering its growth even further. It was not until the late 1960s that the IRA would return on the scene with renewed ferocity.

The Troubles

Duri ng the early to mid-1950s, the IRA performed illegal raids on British weapons depots in order to stockpile arms. IRA rebels would steal weapons from military outposts in the six counties of Northern Ireland, as well as in Britain. They were preparing for an armed campaign called Operation Harvest. The campaign, which was undertaken from 1956 to 1962, was mostly confined to the border that divided the northern and southern parts of Ireland. Designed to harass the British army and increase the pressure for withdrawal from Northern Ireland, the IRA attacked border posts and the military personnel who guarded them.

When its violent border campaign fell short of its goal, the IRA briefly turned its back on violence. Turning its attention back to the "second-class" status of Catholics—and the working class of both faiths—in the north, the group found inspiration in the more peaceful forms of protest sweeping the West during the 1960s.

Equal Rights and Justice

Influenced in part by the growing civil rights movement in the United States, the student riots taking place in Paris and elsewhere in Europe, and the humanitarianism and optimism of the times, the leadership of the IRA began to embrace a socialist agenda, largely based on the theories of German philosopher Karl

Beginning as a student protest in a Parisian suburb, what would become known as *les événements* (the events) quickly spread to a general strike involving ten million French workers (half the French labor force) that paralyzed the French economy for several weeks. This uprising, along with the anti–Vietnam War protests occurring in the United States at the same time, inspired many similar anti-government protests throughout Europe. Even the IRA, long associated with guerrilla warfare, would briefly adopt the more peaceful, though still occasionally violent, tactics of the mass protest.

Marx. Socialism encourages the collective ownership (for example, factories, farms, and stores) of the means of making and selling goods and services. This means that citizens as a united group share ownership of resources and the wealth these resources generate. In theory, there would be no private property and no class distinctions in a socialist society.

During this period, the IRA even abandoned the use of violence as a means of achieving its political goals. The new IRA still pushed for a thirty-two-county, united socialist republic. But its larger goal was to unite Catholics and Protestants throughout the north and south in a workers' revolt against Britain. The IRA struggle was redefined, and it was no longer viewed as Catholics fighting against the Protestants and their British patrons, but oppressed Irish workers of both faiths striving against their British colonial oppressors.

The new idealism of the IRA was not shared by all of its leaders or members, however. Among the IRA ranks were many working-class people who were strongly antisocialist because their lives had been nearly ruined by poverty. To them, a switch to a socialist economy threatened to take away what little they had.

A Return to Arms

The IRA's new pacifist strategy flourished briefly in the 1960s but would be extinguished quickly. In the Northern Ireland counties of Ulster and Derry, nationalist neighborhoods were being attacked by the Royal Ulster Constabulary (RUC; the Protestant-dominated police force of Northern Ireland) and Unionists gangs. Tensions between Catholics and Protestants worsened each day as Catholics continued to press for their civil rights. In addition, both Catholics and Protestants would organize marches through each other's neighborhoods, provocations that often led to street fights, riots, and the calling in of the RUC (who were largely sympathetic to the Protestant, Loyalist community).

By late summer 1969, several Catholic homes had been burned to the ground. Some Catholics were even shot on the streets of

Belfast. Residents of Bogside in Derry, a large Catholic neighbor-
hood, where much of the violence raged, formed a local citizens
army when it became clear that the RUC would not protect them or
their property from attacks by Protestant mobs (including reservists
in the RUC). At this time, the civil and political unrest of Ireland
began to be known as The Troubles. This term is still commonly
used to describe the political situation in Ireland when talking about
the era from the late 1960s to the present.

Protection from harassment by the police, the military, and
Protestant gangs was no longer being provided by the IRA in
these communities, as it had been in the past. Throughout the
1960s, IRA leaders had abandoned planning for future attacks to
turn their attention to larger political ideals. The IRA's strength as
a military organization had been neglected for too long to be able
to react effectively to this wave of attacks. This inability to defend
Catholic neighborhoods led to infighting within the IRA, as certain
militant factions accused the group of losing credibility because it
failed to protect Irish Catholics from brutality.

PIRA

At a convention in December and January 1969–1970, the IRA split
in two over questions of strategy. The IRA's Belfast Brigade
demanded a return to an armed defense of Catholic neighborhoods
in Northern Ireland and a resumption of guerrilla attacks against
British forces. The majority of IRA members, however, voted in
favor of continuing to assert themselves through mainly political
means. The northern brigade walked out of the convention and set
up the Provisional Army Council, which later became the Provisional
Irish Republican Army (PIRA).

A formal split occurred in December 1969 between PIRA and the remaining IRA members, who now called themselves the "Official" IRA and continued to promote a more socialist and pacifist agenda. As a result, on January 11, 1970, Sinn Féin also divided into official and provisional factions.

The Official IRA's Reluctant Return to Violence

Throughout 1970 and 1971, the Official IRA gained support in nationalist districts in Northern Ireland. This support increased with the government's reintroduction of its policy of internment without trial following the arrest of 342 people on August 9, 1971. These people were detained for no other reason than they were known to be sympathetic to the Republican cause. Most were released two days later, but 100 remained in jail, without trial or even any specific charges leveled against them.

In response, IRA volunteers carried out a new campaign of guerrilla attacks against the British army in northern towns. The conflict in Northern Ireland intensified, and thousands of families fled Belfast and Derry. On December 4, 1971, the UVF bombed a Catholic bar in Belfast killing 15 people. In the four months following internment, 114 people—Catholic and Protestant—were killed.

Internment would drag the Official IRA back into the violence it was trying to put behind it. Although IRA chief of staff Cathal Goulding wanted to steer the Official IRA away from the militant republicanism of the PIRA, he felt the group had to respond to the unfair British policy and the ongoing Protestant attacks upon Catholic communities. As a result, it again began to advocate the use of violence to achieve political goals and protest injustice.

British soldiers stand guard near houses that were damaged by IRA bombs fired into the central area of Belfast in August 1971. A new British policy of internment and escalating violence on the part of Protest paramilitary groups against Catholics in Northern Ireland prompted retaliatory attacks like this one by IRA members throughout late 1971. As a result, the Official IRA would soon abandon its recent commitment to finding a peaceful and political solution to the Northern Ireland question.

Bloody Sunday and Its Aftermath

On January 30, 1972, various nationalist factions found themselves reunited at a Sunday march in Derry (known as Londonderry to the Protestant) organized by a Northern Irish Catholic civil rights group. The day would be remembered as Bloody Sunday. During the civil rights demonstration, chaos broke out when some marchers

The IRA's Structure

The Provisional IRA is the largest and best organized of the paramilitary groups currently operating in Ireland. Its day-to-day operations are conducted by a seven-person Army Council, drawn mainly from Northern Ireland and the Irish Republic counties that border the north. The General Army Convention is the supreme authority of the IRA, and it meets only every two years. The convention selects a twelve-member Army Executive that meets every six months. The executive's main task is to select the members of the Army Council and advise the council on all matters concerning the IRA. Army Council decisions are carried out by General Headquarters, which serves as a link between the council and northern and southern commands. Each command has a commanding officer and a director of operations who oversee the IRA cells. Each of these cells is composed of between five and eight members who plan and carry out IRA attacks. There is also a special women's section called Cumann na mBan (Gaelic for "League of Women").

Source: *Frontline: The IRA and Sinn Féin*

began throwing rocks. British soldiers retaliated by firing into the crowd, and thirteen Catholics were killed. The soldiers claimed they were fired on first, while the marchers say the soldiers went on a rampage and shot people in the back as they were fleeing.

A few days later, on February 2, the British Embassy in Dublin was burned down. Three weeks after Bloody Sunday, the Official IRA planted a retaliatory bomb at a British military

British troops take cover behind armored cars as young demonstrators stand in the background on the streets of Derry on Bloody Sunday, January 30, 1972. The soldiers insisted that they had come under sustained gun and bomb attack by members of the IRA and fired only at people in possession of weapons. Those involved in the march and many who witnessed the events testified that none of those killed or injured had any guns or bombs. Inset: A shooting victim is carried away by Irish Catholics on Bloody Sunday.

outpost in Aldershot, England, killing seven people. Three months later, the Official IRA admitted that they were responsible for the death of Ranger William Best, a soldier on leave who was shot in his home in County Derry. Best's murder brought angry protests and calls for the Official IRA to leave Derry. In response, the Official IRA called an absolute cease-fire in May 1972.

The PIRA also called a brief truce with the British army in June 1972. In July, unbeknownst to the Official IRA, they had talks in London with the British government. The PIRA demanded complete withdrawal of Britain from Ireland by 1975. The truce disintegrated after just three days of talks, when the British made it clear that they had no intentions of meeting this demand. Many Republicans suspected the talks were simply designed to distract the IRA and buy time for the planning of British counterterrorism efforts.

In the aftermath of the failed talks, twenty-two PIRA bombs went off in Belfast on July 21, 1972, killing nine people. On the same day, which came to be known as Bloody Friday, a PIRA bomb killed ten people in County Derry. Targets of these bombs included parking garages, bus stations, rail terminals, shops, and homes in Protestant areas. Most of the nineteen dead and dozens of seriously wounded were civilians.

A Splintering Movement

The Official IRA had a huge problem on its hands in 1975. A bitter division had developed between the Official IRA and the Irish National Liberation Army (INLA), another IRA splinter faction. Like the Official IRA, the INLA's goal was the reunification of

Ireland as a socialist republic. The founding INLA members defected from the Official IRA following the 1972 cease-fire, to which they objected. In addition, some members had defected from the PIRA during its cease-fire in 1975. Despite a shared history and socialist agenda, the Official IRA and the INLA were no longer comrades.

Meanwhile, the PIRA was also continuing its violent attacks against both military and civilian targets. In February 1978, a PIRA firebomb exploded in a hotel, killing twelve and injuring twenty-three. On August 27, 1979, a PIRA bomb exploded on the boat of Queen Elizabeth's uncle, Lord Mountbatten, in County Sligo (in the Republic of Ireland), killing him and three other people. On that same day, another bomb exploded in County Down during a PIRA ambush, killing eighteen British soldiers. This was the greatest number of British army casualties inflicted by a Republican group in a single attack since the troubled years between the Easter Rebellion and Partition.

The Official IRA felt that the far less violent campaign that it was waging at the time was more effective militarily and politically, frustrating British forces without terrorizing the public and alienating potential supporters and sympathizers. Their tactics included the blockading of roads throughout the country to make them inaccessible to British troops. They were able to secretly construct these blockades despite the British military's strong presence in cities and throughout the countryside of Northern Ireland. Because of its relatively moderate philosophy and tactics, the Official IRA enjoyed the support of the majority of people in nationalist communities.

Major IRA Attacks

July 21, 1972: Nine people are killed and 130 seriously injured in twenty-two separate explosions in Belfast. Bomb locations included a bus station, a train station, a bank, a pub, a residential street, a strip of shops, and several bridges. The day becomes known as Bloody Friday.

July 31, 1972: Twelve civilians—both Protestant and Catholic—are killed by the explosion of three car bombs in Claudy, County Derry.

February 4, 1974: Twelve people are killed—nine British army members and three civilians—in a bomb attack on an army transport truck in Yorkshire, England.

A paint factory burns in Belfast after being bombed by the IRA in 1972.

November 21, 1974: Twenty civilians are killed in bomb explosions at two pubs in Birmingham, England.

January 17, 1978: Twelve Protestant civilians are killed in a firebomb attack on a restaurant in County Down.

August 27, 1979: Eighteen British army members are killed in two bomb attacks near Warrenpoint, County Down.

July 20, 1982: Eleven British army members are killed in two remote-controlled bomb attacks in London.

February 28, 1985: Nine members of the Royal Ulster Constabulary (RUC) are killed in a mortar bomb attack on an RUC base in Newry, County Down.

November 8, 1987: Eleven people—ten civilians and one RUC member—are killed in a bomb attack in Enniskillen during a Remembrance Day ceremony.

September 22, 1989: Eleven members of the British army are killed in a bomb attack on a British army base in Kent, England.

October 21, 1993: Ten people—nine Protestant civilians and one IRA member—are killed when a bomb goes off prematurely in a fish shop in Belfast.

August 15, 1998: Twenty-nine civilians are killed in a bomb attack in the town center of Omagh, County Tyrone. The splinter group Real IRA claims responsibility. In the face of almost universal outrage and anger, the group apologizes and declares a cease-fire a month later.

Pallbearers carry the casket of Bobby Sands during his funeral on May 7, 1981. Sands was arrested in October 1976, and sentenced to fourteen years imprisonment for his involvement with the IRA. In early 1981, Sands organized a hunger strike among IRA prisoners to protest their status as "ordinary prisoners" rather than political prisoners. He refused food for sixty-six days until he died on May 5, 1981. Over 90,000 people followed Sands's funeral procession to Milltown Cemetery, Belfast, on May 7, 1981.

Counterterrorism

During the 1980s, Britain's counterterrorist campaign shifted toward a new direction. Rather than focusing only on preventing attacks by rounding up suspected IRA members, it would now also try to break the spirit of those in custody through long and extremely harsh prison terms. It was also hoped that the harsh treatment of IRA prisoners would make other Irish Catholics think twice before joining the group and taking part in its operations.

Before 1976, IRA members who were arrested had received a special category status—they were considered prisoners of war, a designation that gave them some legal protection under the 1949 Geneva Convention (an international agreement signed by over 150 countries, including Britain, that forbids the physical and psychological mistreatment of prisoners of war). This special category for IRA prisoners was abolished in 1976, and five years later the British government introduced a strict criminalization policy. Under this new policy, mere membership in the IRA was a criminal offense, whether or not the member had actively committed a crime, such as bombing a target or planning to do so. Suspected IRA members underwent trials without juries; a lone judge decided the prisoners' fates and often handed out lengthy sentences. Convicted IRA members were brought to "interrogation centers," where many claimed to have been tortured.

Hunger Strikes

Imprisoned IRA members vowed not to buckle under this strategy. Instead, on March 1, 1981, several of them began a hunger strike. The strike, which lasted more than seven months, resulted

Young supporters of IRA prisoner Bobby Sands paste posters bearing his image on a rooftop. His death following a two-month hunger strike in prison provoked riots in Northern Ireland and street protests in many cities around the world. By the time the hunger strike ended on October 3, 1981, ten men had starved themselves to death.

in the deaths of ten Irish Republicans. The horror of the hunger strike, which was followed with great interest around the globe, led to the collapse of the British criminalization policy and renewed support for the IRA among many Irish Catholics worldwide. Bobby Sands, the first hunger striker to die, was elected to the British Parliament while on strike. His participation in the strike created a tide of popular support, and though he would not live to either regain his freedom or take his seat in Parliament, his election was a huge symbolic victory for the Republican cause. Riots broke out in both Northern Ireland and the Republic of Ireland following Sands's death, and close to 100,000 people attended his funeral in May 1981.

A New Direction, a New Hope

While Bobby Sands's death in some ways seemed like a demoralizing low point for Irish Republicans, the hunger strikes also invigorated the movement and increased Republicans' desire to rid Northern Ireland of Britain's presence.

The Republican movement received a new jolt of energy, as well, with a change of leadership. In 1983, Sinn Féin selected civil rights activist Gerry Adams as its president. Adams, born and raised in Belfast, grew up in a working-class Catholic family that suffered routine discrimination and severe economic hardship. After completing his schooling, Adams became involved with the struggle for civil rights and joined Sinn Féin. As a result of his controversial political activities, he was jailed without trial by the British during most of the 1970s.

Adams was a well-liked and respected political activist and a popular figure throughout Catholic Ireland. His election to the presidency of Sinn Féin gave the group more legitimacy than it enjoyed before. As a result, it gained more power to accomplish its goals, earned many election victories, and became a force that the British had to work with and acknowledge. His popularity also gave him the leverage among Republicans to finally steer Sinn Féin and the IRA toward the peace table. A less charismatic and beloved figure would have met with more sharp resistance from Republican hard-liners.

The oldest of ten children, Gerry Adams was born on October 6, 1948, in a working-class area of West Belfast. He continues to reside there with his wife and son. After finishing school in the 1960s, Gerry worked as a bartender while becoming increasingly involved in the Catholic civil rights movement in Northern Ireland. In 1983, he was elected president of Sinn Féin.

The Rocky Path to Peace

Irish Catholic voters were increasingly uncomfortable with Sinn Féin's apparent connection to a violent terrorist group that was responsible for the deaths of dozens of innocent civilians. The IRA's continued use of violence was also leading to the exclusion of Sinn Féin from any official discussions of Northern Ireland's future. Under this popular and political pressure, the PIRA declared a cease-fire on August 31, 1994. This allowed Sinn Féin to join other legislative groups in talks that led to the Good Friday Agreement of 1998.

The path to the agreement was a tortured one, however. The peace talks were sponsored by the governments of Britain and the Republic of Ireland, and were to include both Unionist and Republican groups. Initially, Unionists refused to participate in any talks that included Sinn Féin members. Aside from the age-old distrust and hatred between the two sides, the main sticking point was the IRA's refusal to decommission (put beyond use or destroy) its weapons before beginning peace talks. The IRA viewed decommissioning before a deal was struck as surrender, feeling it would take away what little bargaining power it had.

Former U.S. senator George Mitchell was then asked to head a separate group that would try to resolve the decommissioning issue. In January 1996, the group published its report, recommending that decommissioning should take place during negotiations and that all parties involved in the talks should commit themselves to democratic principles and the rejection of violence. Five days later, the IRA ended its cease-fire by exploding a bomb in London's Canary Wharf, killing two people.

The British and Irish governments soldiered on, setting a date for multiparty talks but denying Sinn Féin the right to participate as long as the IRA continued to embrace violence. Without Sinn Féin's participation, however, the talks were meaningless. Another IRA bomb exploded in a Manchester, England, shopping center in February 1996. The slim and fragile chance for peace that had briefly appeared seemed to have been extinguished.

Former U.S. senator George Mitchell *(center)*, Canadian general John De Chastelain *(left)*, and former prime minister of Finland Hari Holkeri *(right)*, the three members of the Northern Ireland Peace Process International Arms Commission, sit for a press conference in Belfast on January 24, 1996. On that day, they unveiled the commission's report that advised the British government to drop its demand that the IRA lay down its arms before being permitted to take part in the all-party talks on Northern Ireland's future.

With the election on May 1, 1997, in Britain of Tony Blair's Liberal government, after almost two decades of Conservative rule, the IRA sensed that chances for progress in Northern Ireland were greater now than ever. On July 20, 1997, it again declared a cease-fire and was readmitted to the multiparty peace talks. The talks began on September 15, 1997, and eventually led to the Good Friday Agreement of April 10, 1998 (so-called because it was signed on the Friday before Easter).

The Good Friday Agreement

The Good Friday Agreement was a plan for Northern Ireland that would allow the province to be ruled by a democratically elected assembly of both Unionist and Republican members, with a minimum of influence from London. A north/south council of ministers would be created to encourage greater contacts and cooperation between the Republic of Ireland and Northern Ireland. Similarly, a British-Irish Intergovernmental Conference would be created to forge greater cooperation between Britain and the Republic of Ireland.

On the thorny issue of Northern Ireland's union with either Britain or Ireland, the Good Friday Agreement leaves the decision to majority rule. In the short term, most people in Northern Ireland wish to remain within the United Kingdom, and that majority opinion will be respected. If, however, opinion shifts, referendums will be held in both Ireland and Northern Ireland to determine if the "two Irelands" should be united. In the meantime, Ireland must amend its constitution to drop its territorial claim to Northern Ireland.

The agreement also established the Northern Ireland Human Rights Commission designed to protect minorities from discrimination. A Victims Commission would also be established to promote reconciliation between Catholics and Protestants and preserve the memory of the 3,600 people killed in Ireland, Northern Ireland, and Britain since 1969.

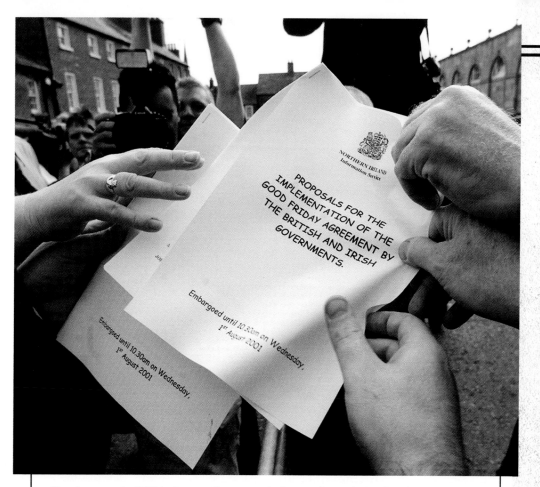

On August 1, 2001, journalists reach for copies of the British and Irish governments' proposals for how best to implement (put into place) the terms of the Good Friday Agreement reached three years earlier between Northern Ireland's Protestant and Catholic political parties. The British and Irish proposals attempted to further ongoing peace talks by addressing the issues of the disarmament of paramilitary groups (Protestant and Catholic), police reform and security, and the reduction of the number of British troops in Northern Ireland.

In an area bristling with weapons and combatants, the issue of creating and preserving the peace was especially sensitive. All sides needed to feel they were not being left exposed by laying down their arms, so each party had to yield something. All the weapons of Republican and Loyalist paramilitary groups would have to be handed over within two years of implementation of the agreement. The British army's presence in the province would be greatly reduced if conditions allowed. Northern Ireland's security arrangements would return to a peacetime footing. The RUC police force, long staffed by Loyalist-sympathizers, would be transformed to reflect the makeup of the entire community. Finally, the release of prisoners convicted of terrorist offenses would be sped up, with all prisoners (except for those belonging to groups that had not declared a cease-fire) being freed within two years of the agreement's enactment.

The Good Friday Agreement went into effect in May 2000, and a power-sharing government composed of Republicans and Unionists, Catholics and Protestants, was elected and now governs Northern Ireland. The government remains shaky, however, and has been shut down twice due to conflicts between the Ulster Unionist Party (UUP) and Sinn Féin. The IRA continues to be accused of organizing riots and stashing arms, and the leader of the UUP is under constant pressure from party members to pull out of any government that includes Sinn Féin. The prospects for enduring peace and cooperation in Northern Ireland remain highly uncertain, chances made no better by the existence of still-active Catholic and Protestant splinter groups.

The Real IRA's Threat to Peace

Predictably, the peace process set in motion by the Good Friday Agreement was not accepted by all nationalist factions. Several official IRA leaders abandoned the IRA in late 1997 in opposition to Sinn Féin's acceptance of George Mitchell's decommissioning recommendations.

A new group that called itself the Real IRA grew out of opposition to the 1994 and 1997 PIRA cease-fires, as well as Sinn Féin's support of the Good Friday Agreement. The Real IRA began to fill its ranks with disgruntled ex-members of other IRA factions. The group quickly gained a reputation for extreme violence and ruthlessness.

The Real IRA is responsible for what is widely considered the single worst act of violence of The Troubles—the Omagh car bomb, detonated on a Saturday afternoon in the busy downtown of Omagh, County Tyrone, in August 1998. The Omagh bomb killed twenty-nine people and injured more than a hundred.

The Real IRA had already carried out a series of other terrorist attacks: Earlier in 1998, it bombed the downtown areas of Moira and Portadown, both in County Armagh, Northern Ireland. And just two weeks before the Omagh attack, the Real IRA planted a 500-pound bomb in another crowded shopping area, this one in Banbridge, County Down, injuring thirty-three civilians and two police officers.

The public outrage—both Catholic and Protestant—over the Omagh attack was so intense that the Real IRA was forced to issue a statement just days after the attack, saying that it would suspend all further military operations. Gerry Adams, attempting to distance Sinn Féin from the Real IRA's actions, declared that violence must be a thing of the past. Senior IRA officials visited the homes of those members who were thought to be involved in the Omagh bombing and urged them to cease their activities. It is thought, however, that neither Sinn Féin nor the old guard IRA has much, if any, influence over the Real IRA.

American Support of the IRA

It has long been thought that Irish American citizens provide the bulk of the IRA's funding, through contributions to so-called charitable organizations that are actually a front for the paramilitary group. Over 40 million Americans claim Irish ancestry, and in cities such as New York, Boston, and Chicago, which have large Irish Catholic populations (and still receive thousands of Irish immigrants a year), pro-Republican and anti-British sentiments can be very strong.

One charitable group, in particular, the Irish Northern Aid Committee (Noraid), has been accused of funding the IRA and even shipping arms to the paramilitary group. Its leaders say that the charity was founded in 1969 to offer financial assistance to the families of IRA members jailed or killed in the struggle against Britain. They deny any relationship to the IRA and claim that the money they raise is distributed through Sinn Féin in Dublin and the Green Cross (a charitable trust for families of IRA members) in Belfast. In 1977, the U.S. Department of Justice forced Noraid to officially register as an agent of the Provisional IRA.

The Real IRA cease-fire did not last. Many attacks in Northern Ireland and Britain since early 2000 can be traced back to the Real IRA, such as the September 2000 bomb hurled at British intelligence headquarters and the March 2001 bomb planted outside the BBC Television Network headquarters, both in London. In May 2001, the United States government officially designated the Real IRA as a terrorist organization.

Other Paramilitary Threats

The Real IRA is joined in its terrorism activities by the INLA and the Continuity IRA. All three are committed to fighting against any settlement that does not create a thirty-two-county Ireland.

In addition, Protestant paramilitary groups continue to launch violent attacks in Northern Ireland. While most Protestant groups have maintained a cease-fire since October 1994, the Orange Volunteers and the Red Hand Defenders have declared their intention, according to the British Broadcasting Corporation, not to "stand idly by and watch as our culture, heritage, and religion are attacked and destroyed before our eyes." The Orange Volunteers, in particular, have claimed responsibility for several murders and bombings since the signing of the Good Friday Agreement, including the assassination of a prominent Catholic human-rights lawyer, Rosemary Nelson.

A New Beginning

Despite the ongoing violent activities of the Real IRA, the INLA, the Continuity IRA, and various Protestant paramilitary groups, the old-guard IRA offered a ray of hope for the weary Catholic and Protestant residents of Northern Ireland on July 18, 2002. In an unprecedented statement, it offered its "sincere apologies and condolences" for the 1,800 people (650 of them civilians) killed during its thirty-year campaign against the British.

The statement ended with the declaration, "The IRA is committed unequivocally to the search for freedom, justice, and peace in Ireland." Coming just three days before the thirtieth anniversary of Bloody Friday, Catholics and Protestants alike fervently hoped this apology and commitment to peace was indeed sincere.

Conclusion

In all eras throughout history, violence has been used for political gain by both rulers and the people who opposed them. This has been particularly true of Ireland's troubled past. The tradition of armed resistance to British military and political occupation of Ireland is a long, tragic one. Many people have lost their lives trying to reunite the thirty-two counties of Ireland. Many have died trying to maintain a union with England. And many innocent people have been killed as a result of this political agitation. For more than 400 years, violence has been a frequently recurring theme in the lives of Irish citizens. Today, Northern Ireland is enjoying a fragile state of peace. But the bloody cycle of terrorism and police and military counterterrorism can hardly be called a thing of the past yet.

Substantial change to the hostile politics that set the violent tone of Northern Ireland society is needed if the Good Friday Agreement—or any similar type of agreement, cease-fire, or peace treaty—is to provide a permanent solution to The Troubles. Yet several years after the agreement went into effect, the poor communities of Northern Ireland that suffered the most throughout the conflicts remain suspended between bloody battle and a tense cease-fire.

The fundamental problems of Ireland persist. Should Northern Ireland remain in a union with Britain? Will there ever be a whole and united Ireland? Will the Catholic citizens of Northern Ireland ever achieve true equality with their Protestant neighbors? Will they be treated with fairness and justice and

Catholic children play with toy guns under an IRA mural in the mostly Catholic Markets area of South Belfast on August 14, 2001. While real guns remain in abundance in both Catholic and Protestant neighborhoods throughout Northern Ireland, the IRA began decommissioning (permanently putting beyond use) its weapons in October 2001, a process it continued to pursue in 2002.

Sinn Féin president Gerry Adams *(second from left)* delivers a speech on Easter Sunday, March 31, 2002. The occasion was the commemoration of the eighty-sixth anniversary of the 1916 Easter Rebellion, a failed uprising against British troops that occurred in the streets of Dublin and included members of what would later evolve into the IRA. Adams's address was given in Glasnevin Cemetery, Dublin, before a monument to the Irish who died fighting for the Republican cause throughout the years.

equal opportunity in their own land? Will Catholics and Protestants ever live together as true neighbors, rather than warring tribes? Will the men, women, and children of Northern Ireland—both Catholic and Protestant—ever feel safe in their homes and streets? Or will they continue to live in terrified anticipation of the next bomb blast, the next bullet through the window? While the answers to these questions remain to be seen, the choices for Northern Ireland's future, are now, more than ever before, in the hands of the people.

Glossary

absentee landlord   A proprietor who lives away from his or her estate.

agenda   An underlying plan or program, often ideological or political.

cell   The basic and usually smallest unit of a terrorist group.

cessation   A temporary or final ending of a certain action.

clan   Group composed of a number of families who claim descent from a common ancestor.

colonialism   Enforced control by one power over a dependent area or people.

decommission   To remove from service or make inactive.

deploy   To extend or place a military unit in battle formation or other appropriate positions; to spread out, utilize, or arrange strategically.

detain   To hold or keep in custody; to restrain from proceeding.

evict   To remove a tenant by legal process or physical force.

front   A person, group, or thing used to mask the identity, true character, or activity of the controlling agent.

guerrilla   A person who engages in irregular warfare, especially as a member of an independent group carrying out acts of harassment or sabotage against government forces or other political targets.

immigrate   To enter a country that is not your own and take up permanent residence there.

internment   To confine, jail, or impound, especially during a war.

martial law   The law administered by military forces that is invoked by a government in an emergency if it fears mass protests and opposition or if civilian law enforcement agencies are unable to maintain public order and safety.

militant   (n) Someone engaged in warfare or combat; (adj.) to be aggressively active on behalf of a certain cause.

paramilitary   A fighting unit organized like a military force but not part of a nation's official primary army.

retaliation   Getting revenge for a specific act; getting back at someone.

revolutionary   (n) One involved in a revolution; a believer in revolutionary doctrines; (adj.) constituting or bringing about a major or fundamental change.

socialism   Any of various economic and political theories encouraging public ownership and control of the means of production and distribution of goods.

sovereignty   Supreme power over a region, or freedom from outside control.

terrorism   A systematic use of terror, especially as a means of political persuasion.

For More Information

American Irish Historical Society
991 Fifth Avenue
New York, NY 10028
(212) 288-2263
Web site: http://www.aihs.org

Amnesty International Irish Section
Sean MacBride House
48 Fleet Street
Dublin 2, Ireland
011-353 1 677 6361
Web site: http://www.amnesty.ie

Amnesty International USA
322 8th Avenue
New York, NY 10001
(212) 807-8400
Web site: http://www.amnesty-usa.org

Co-operation Ireland
20 Herbert Place
Dublin 2, Ireland
011-353 1 661 0588
Web site: http://www.cooperationireland.org

European Union Special Support Programme for Peace and
 Reconciliation in Northern Ireland and the Border Counties
 of Ireland
McAuley House
2-14 Castle Street
Belfast, Northern Ireland BT1 1SA
011-44-28 9034 8195
Web site: http://www.eu-peace.org

Irish Cultural Centre
200 New Boston Drive
P.O. Box 246
Canton, MA 02021
(781) 821-8291
Web site: http://www.irishculture.org

The Mediation Network for Northern Ireland
10 Upper Crescent
Belfast, Northern Ireland BT7 1NT
011-44-028 90 438614
Web site: http://www.mediation-network.org.uk

Web Sites

Due to the changing nature of Internet links, the Rosen
Publishing Group, Inc., has developed an online list of Web sites
related to the subject of this book. This site is updated regularly.
Please use this link to access the list:

http://www.rosenlinks.com/iwmito/ira/

For Further Reading

Banting, Erinn. *Ireland: The Land* (Lands, Peoples, and Cultures). Ontario, Canada: Crabtree Publishers, 2002.

Bartoletti, Susan Campbell. *Black Potatoes: The Story of the Great Irish Famine, 1845–1850*. New York: Houghton Mifflin, 2001.

Conroy, John. *Belfast Diary: War as a Way of Life*. Boston: Beacon Press, 1995.

Fridell, Ron. *Terrorism: Political Violence at Home and Abroad* (Issues in Focus). Hillside, NJ: Enslow Publishers, 2001.

Lyons, Mary E., ed. *Feed the Children First: Irish Memories of the Great Hunger*. New York: Atheneum Publishers, 2002.

Lyons, Mary E. *Knockabeg: A Famine Tale*. New York: Houghton Mifflin, 2001.

Stewart, Gail B. *Terrorism* (Understanding Issues). San Diego: Kidhaven Press, 2002.

Toolis, Kevin. *Rebel Hearts: Journeys Within the IRA's Soul*. New York: St. Martin's Press, 1996.

Wagner, Heather Lehr. *The IRA and England*. Broomall, PA: Chelsea House, 2002.

Wilson, Laura (Illustrator). *How I Survived the Irish Famine: The Journal of Mary O'Flynn* (Time Travelers). New York: HarperCollins, 2001.

Bibliography

BBC News. 2002. "The Search for Peace." Retrieved June 2002 (http://news.bbc.co.uk/hi/english/static/northern_ireland/ understanding/default.stm).

Associated Press. "Politicians Intervene in N. Ireland." *New York Times*. June 26, 2002. Retrieved June 2002 (http://www. nytimes.com/aponline/international/AP-Northern-Ireland.html).

Beresford, David. *Ten Men Dead: The Story of the 1981 Irish Hunger Strike*. New York: Atlantic Monthly Press, 1997.

Boyne, Sean. "Uncovering the Irish Republican Army." Frontline Online (reprinted from *Jane's Intelligence Review*). August 1, 1996. Retrieved June 2002 (http://www.pbs.org/wgbh/ pages/frontline/shows/ira/inside/org.html).

CAIN Web Service. "Chronology of Major Violent Incidents, 1969–1998." March 13, 2002. Retrieved June 2002 (http://cain.ulst.ac.uk/issues/violence/chronmaj.htm).

CNN Student News. "IRA 'Sorry' for Civilian Deaths." July 18, 2002. Retrieved August 2002 (http://fyi.cnn.com/2002/fyi/ 07/18/ira.apology).

Coogan, Tim Pat. *The IRA*. New York: Palgrave Macmillan, 2002.

Coogan, Tim Pat. *The Troubles: Ireland's Ordeal and the Search for Peace*. New York: Palgrave Macmillan, 2002.

Donnelly, James S., Jr. *The Great Irish Potato Famine*. London: Sutton Publishing, 2001.

Bibliography

Gallagher, Thomas. *Paddy's Lament: Ireland, 1846–1847: Prelude to Hatred*. New York: Harvest Books, 1987.

Golway, Terry. *For the Cause of Liberty: A Thousand Years of Ireland's Heroes*. New York: Simon & Schuster, 2000.

Holland, Jack. *Hope Against History: The Course of Conflict in Northern Ireland*. New York: Henry Holt and Co., Inc., 1999.

"The Irish Republican Army and the Armed Struggle in Irish Politics." Web article. 1998. Retrieved July 2002 (http://users.westnet.gr/~cgian/irahist.htm).

Kee, Robert. *The Green Flag: A History of Irish Nationalism*. New York: Penguin USA, 2001.

Laxton, Edward. *The Famine Ships: The Irish Exodus to America*. New York: Henry Holt and Co., Inc., 1998.

Llywelyn, Morgan. *A Pocket History of Irish Rebels*. Dublin, Ireland: The O'Brien Press, 2000.

McKittrick, David, and David McVea. *Making Sense of the Troubles: The Story of the Conflict in Northern Ireland*. New York: New Amsterdam Books, 2002.

Miller, Kerby A. *Emigrants and Exiles: Ireland and the Irish Exodus to North America*. New York: Oxford University Press, 1988.

O'Brien, Brendan. *The Long War: The IRA and Sinn Fein*. Syracuse, NY: Syracuse University Press, 1999.

Washington Post. "A Time Line for the Troubles." 1998. Retrieved June 2002. (http://www.washingtonpost.com/wp-srv/inatl/longterm/nireland/timeline.htm).

Woodham-Smith, Cecil. *The Great Hunger: Ireland, 1845–1849*. New York: Penguin USA, 1995.

Index

About the Author

Susie Derkins is a folk artist who lives in New York City. This is her sixth book for the Rosen Publishing Group, Inc.

Photo Credits

Cover © Chris Lisle/Corbis; pp. 1, 5 © TimePix; pp. 6, 47 © Paul MrErlane/Corbis; p. 9 © Michael St. Maur Sheil/Corbis; pp. 11, 13, 16–17, 17 (inset), 20, 23, 26, 30, 32–33, 33 (inset), 41 © Hulton/ Archive/Getty Images; p. 36 © Leif Skoogfors/Corbis; pp. 38–39, 43 © Corbis; p. 45 © Paul MrErlane/AP/Wide World Photos; p. 53 © Peter Morrison/AP/Wide World Photos; p. 54 © John Cogill/ AP/Wide World Photos.

Series Design and Layout

Nelson Sá